I0098195

VIA Folios 131

Missing Madonnas

Other Books by Gil Fagiani

Crossing 116th Street, Skidrow Penthouse (2004)
Rooks, Rain Mountain Press (2007)
Grandpa's Wine, Poets Wear Prada (2008)
A Blanquito in El Barrio, Rain Mountain Press (2009)
Chianti in Connecticut, Bordighera Press (2010)
Serfs of Psychiatry, Finishing Line Press (2012)
Stone Walls, Bordighera Press (2014)
Logos, Guernica Editions (2015)

Missing Madonnas

Gil Fagiani

BORDIGHERA PRESS

Library of Congress Control Number: 2018947176

© 2018 by Gil Fagiani

Copy editor: Cindy Hochman
Author Photo: David Gonzalez
Front Cover design: Nicholas Grosso

All rights reserved. Parts of this book may be reprinted only by written permission from the author, and may not be reproduced for publication in book, magazine, or electronic media of any kind, except for purposes of literary review by critics.

Printed in the United States.

Published by
BORDIGHERA PRESS
John D. Calandra Italian American Institute
25 West 43rd Street, 17th Floor
New York, NY 10036

VIA FOLIOS 131
ISBN 978-1-59954-135-8

CONTENTS

Postscript

Musical Sources

Acknowledgments

About the Author

I am honored and proud to shepherd this book through its final stages *per il mio fagiano, mia anima gemella in amore, vita e poesia negli ultimi 36 anni e per l'eternità* and in his mother's Sicilian, *pi lu miu faggianu, mia anima gemella in amuri, vita e puisia nall'ultimi 36 anni e pi l'eternità*—for my pheasant, my soulmate in love, life, and poetry for the past 36 years and into eternity.

Maria Lisella

I dedicate this book to my mother,
Benedetta "Tina" Fiocco Fagiani,
who instilled in me a love for the written word.

LU CANTE—THE SONG*

A chi nen cante chiù si fa sciapite
                    lu sense de la vite.
A chi chiù cante pijje chiù sapore
                    la voce de lu core.

—Cesare Fagiani**

THE SONG

To those who no longer sing, the spirit of life
                    is tasteless.
To those who sing more, the voice of the heart
                    gets more flavor.

---

*   Translated from Lancianese (Abruzzese) dialect into English by Gil Fagiani, with the assistance of Professor Luigi Bonaffini

**   A cousin of Gil's, Cesare Fagiani (1901—1965) was born in the medieval city of Lanciano and was considered one of Abruzzo's leading poets from the 1930s to the 1960s. In 1992, after Gil translated a poem from Italian to English by Cesare's wife, Candida Di Santo Fagiani, ending with the line *tutta Poesia*—everything is poetry—Gil began to write poetry.

BAD BREAD

LUNAR ARRIVAL

Los Angeles, June 24, 1945

Mom's belly, swollen
as the full moon above.

An earthquake rumbles,
her neighbor, the wife-beater,
rushes her to the hospital
in a battered pickup truck.

The sheet music
to a melancholy tune
that found a name
—my birth certificate.

TESTA ROSSA—REDHEAD

Abruzzo, Italy

Red hair tucked into a bun, she bicycles
three kilometers from Frascara to
Fagnano Alto to teach the farmers' children.

She calls *three* Dante's number
and uses three levels of persuasion
to cure her pupils' tendency toward error.
First, she peels the bark off a *grignale*
branch, hard and flexible as a car antenna,
and whips miscreants' hands, palms up.

Those who persist in their blunders
must kneel for hours on *sassolini
di breccia*—hard-edged little stones.

The hardcore recalcitrants
she outfits with a cardboard sign
reading *Sono un somaro*—*I am a jackass.*

Two of her star students drag
the guilty party in front of their family's house
with a rope around their neck,

while the rest of the class marches
behind in solemn procession, chanting
Hee-haw! Hee-haw! Hee-haw!

The farmers applaud *Testa Rossa*,
boast that her students earn the highest
test scores in all Fagnano Alto.

THE MISSING MADONNA

On the night of October 22, 1598, a pilgrim entered Count Joppolo's castle, in the seacoast village of Capo d'Orlando, Sicily—then governed by the city of Naso—and blew a *buccina*, a brass instrument used to warn of the arrival of pirates. When the Count and his guards reproached the pilgrim, he departed, leaving a cloth sack containing a *statuina*—little statue—of the Madonna cradling *Bambino Gesù* in her arms. A sanctuary was built on the former site of the Count's hilltop castle. The Madonna's image was of extraordinary beauty, and over the years would be credited with the miraculous healing of children stricken with smallpox, driving away foreign invaders, protecting ships buffeted by stormy seas, and saving from drowning Pietro Giron, the Viceroy of Sicily, who had fallen into a cistern. On the night of December 12, 1925, the very night that the *Orlandini*—the townspeople—were celebrating the city of Capo d'Orlando's independence from Naso, sacrilegious hands stole the sacred *statuina*. Later, a substitute was made and put in her place. Over the years, the *Orlandini* have mounted numerous campaigns to recover the original Madonna. Recently, they've produced postcards and postmarks with messages of faith in order to sustain yet another campaign to find their Blessed Mother.

BAD BREAD

It was during the First World War
and the bread was bad.
With little wheat to work with,
the bakeries of Capo d'Orlando
stretched out what they had
by adding *sassi in polvere*—powdered stones—
to the loaves they baked.

Only Raffaela held out,
using the higher-priced *puro grano*
to make bread that tasted like bread
instead of cardboard and dust.

Not wanting to see her neighbors starve,
she gave out too much bread on credit,
so by the end of the war, between people
unable to pay their debts
and the inflated cost of flour,
the store went under.

The legend of her grandmother's
bottega—dry goods store—
lived on in my mother's mind,
and whenever she was asked about
the social situation
of her ancestors in Sicily,
she insisted they weren't poor
pescatori e contadini
—fishermen and field hands—
but middle-class shopkeepers.

ADDIO—FAREWELL

Capo d'Orlando, Sicily, 1922

Everyone in our seacoast town
begins to cry
when they hear we're leaving.

The priest takes us to visit
the Black Madonna of Tindari
to ask for her blessings.

The night before we leave,
we roast chestnuts, sip
Marsala, sing childhood songs.

After Mass, the whole town
flocks around us, stroking
our hair, pinching our cheeks.

Sobs echo off ancient walls
as we lumber to our bus
dragging cardboard suitcases.

People hand us cheese,
salami, hard-boiled eggs,
pictures of San Cono.

Cousin Carmela tries
to squat in front of the bus
to keep us from departing.

Doors close, heads down
like *girasoli*—sunflowers—
in the dusk, a slow descent.

HIS FEET ARE HIS MOTHER'S

At five,
Angeletto suffers a stroke.
By fifteen,
he can no longer walk or talk.
His mother carries him to school
on her shoulders
up and down
two hundred marble steps.

A paved street of 600 feet
would do the trick,
but the full-time fisherman,
part-time mayor
says he can't conquer
the *lentezza*—the slowness—
of bureaucratic procedures
to raise the cash for the road.

"What can I do?" Angeletto's
mother asks. "Leave him
in the house all day like a cripple?"
A friend counsels,
"Put him in an *instituto*."
"No, chickens and pigs
are locked up all day," she says,
"not a smart boy like my son
whose teacher built him
a special computer
to talk to his friends by email."

Angeletto's ninety pounds
bends his mother in two.
"I'm not asking for much,"
she tells anybody who will listen,

"but *un pezzettino di strada*
—a little piece of road."

HUNGER

shadowed the hilltop towns
of Sicily after the war.

When the packet arrived Christmas week,
the Giacomelli family of ten
blessed their relatives in America
for their kindness, *generosità*.

With fumbling fingers
they peeled off the brown packing,
removed coffee, sugar, cornmeal, flour,
and a glass jar filled with gray powder.

That week, much bread,
cake, and coffee were consumed,
and when nothing was left but the jar,
92-year-old Attilio Giacomelli mixed
the powder with milk, and ate it as porridge.

Not long after New Year's, the letter arrived
from Ninfa, Attilio's niece,
telling him of his brother Giovanni's death
and his wish to have his ashes
scattered across the land where he was born.

L'AMERICA

MELTING POTTY

In civics class, Giovanna waves her hands.
"What is it, Jean?"
"I gotta use the backa-house."
"How many times do I have to tell you,
we say *bathroom*, not *back-house*?"
"Please," Giovanna says, her hands
pressed together in praying mode. "I gotta go."
"Up front," the teacher says.
Giovanna knows the routine.
She lowers herself onto her hands
and kneels in front of the class.
"Please, please, can I use the bat-room?"
The students titter.
"That's enough," the teacher snaps.
"It's the only way I can get these people
to talk without using their hands."

THE BLACK HAND

West Village, 1921

Extortion threats
slipped under the door

of anyone with a job.
A police leaflet

tacked to the wall
of a charred storefront.

L'AMERICA

West 3rd Street, Manhattan, 1926

Cuncetta lays out trays
of crushed tomatoes
to be dried on her fire escape.
She's making Sunday sauce
for her husband's family:
fifteen mouths of perpetual hunger.

Above, Enza holds a spray bottle
her mother uses when ironing.
She sprays out the window,
watching droplets gleam in the sunlight,
laughs when a gust of wind blows
water in her face.

"*Hoooh! Assassino! Assassino!*"
Cuncetta bellows, as Enza's mother
runs into the room. "*Ch'è successo?*"
she says, sticking her head out the window.

"My tomatoes are being ruined
by one of your brats," Cuncetta yells.
"*Mannaggia l'America!*"—Damn America!
—Enza's mother cries.

Why did my husband drag me
to this infernal place, far from
my village, with its soothing sounds
of sea waves and church bells,
its lemon orchards and honey lumps
of figs, away from Papà and Mamma,
my brothers and sisters.

She stamps her feet, bites her knuckles,
grabs the bottle out of Enza's hands,
slapping her in the arms, face, legs,
leaving her to whimper all afternoon
in a corner of the hallway.

AUNT LIA

G randpa called her Lia, after his godmother: Rosalia. Her dark eyes burned like his when she heard Caruso sing "*E Lucevan Le Stelle*" from Puccini's *Tosca*. When she was six, Grandpa decided to cultivate her passion for music; bought a Steinway and hired a teacher who came from Florence to give her private lessons. In high school, Lia mastered Chopin's études, polonaises, nocturnes; dazzled audiences in recitals all over town. At the same time, Grandpa became a celebrity in the Italian community, designing fur coats for luminaries like Rosa Ponselle, leading soprano of her time. Lia escorted Grandpa to banquets and fashion shows, and *paesani* flocked to their dinner parties, where Lia performed for them. At one soirée, she played Chopin's *Nocturne in D-flat major* so *dolcissimo*, it left the audience in tears, including an impresario who hosted a weekly radio show. Two days later, Lia received a letter from him offering her a job in his radio orchestra, working in New York, Philadelphia, Boston. Brimming with excitement, she showed the letter to her biggest fan—her father. Rather than smile, he ranted, "No daughter of mine is going to stay in a hotel or work full-time as long as I'm alive." Lia begged him to reconsider, but the more she begged, the more obstinate he grew, until he lost control. "*Basta* ! I bought your piano and I can chop it into firewood!" That night, Lia played Chopin's *Nocturne in D-flat major* with such *tenerezza* that Grandpa came into the room and patted her on the shoulder. He apologized for his outburst and pleaded for her forgiveness, and for her return to the old routine of playing for friends and at local recitals. Slowly, she closed her keyboard and never played again.

ZA' CANDIDA SAYS

drinking wine
fa sangue—makes blood,

pisciando—pissing—on a cut
helps heal it.

The life force flows
in and out.

AMERICAN NOW

Looking down
from the elevated line
of the Sixth Avenue subway
Tina watches the dark streets
of Greenwich Village vanish
into Old World memories.

She is happy to go
happy to speed away
from Mamma's
nervous eyes
and Sicilian war cries
away from alleyways
reeking
of fruit and fish
and guinea stinker cigars
away from pinching cousins
bristly moustaches
and barber shops
buzzing
with the babble
of a dozen dago dialects.

Tina speaks American now
smells American now
looks American now.

The sole sign
of her immigrant home:
the pierced
gold heart earrings
her grandmother
sent her from Messina
she throws
out the subway window.

ROSA MOVES FROM THE VILLAGE TO VILLA AVENUE

I was born on 3rd Street in the West Village, when it was swarming with Italian immigrants. We lived on the second floor, close to the Sixth Avenue elevated subway line, and sometimes Papà would wave at me from inside the train on his way back from work. Across the street was a horse barn that reeked of manure. Down below was a speakeasy where there were constant fights and police raids. Once, somebody was murdered and I saw the bloodstains on the sidewalk. We shared a bathroom in the hallway with Grazia, whose son was a drug addict. Often I saw foam dripping from his mouth. When my father landed a job at the Kingsbridge Veterans Hospital, we moved to a new building on Villa Avenue in the Bronx, where we had our own bathroom. Soon, Cousin Maria was coming by every Saturday to bathe her kids, which infuriated Mamma. I remember the day we moved in. Papà was at work and a huge rat scurried across the living room floor. My sisters and I screamed our heads off, while Mamma closed the windows, cornered the rat, and beat it to death with a broom. The next day, one of the 12 kids of a poor fisherman held the dead rat by the tail and chased after me. Neighbors claimed that goats roamed along Jerome Avenue, a block away. When my cousins found out, they called us the "Nanny Goat Cousins."

LA VITA

There's never enough
macaroni.

You never do enough
for Mamma.

Two maxims—
one way of life.

MOM'S MEMORY

P.S. 80, Bronx, 1932

"They're all greaseballs," Miss Donahue
hisses to Miss Dailey, glaring at Dom,

Vinnie, Pasquale, Luigi, Nino,
roughhousing in the hallway.

Tina flashes her dark eyes.
"We didn't mean you," Miss Donahue says.

VISIONS

Anselmo Ricci survived
the sinking of the *Andrea Doria*
but lost his brother, sister-in-law,
a niece, two nephews, and
a pet Neapolitan Mastiff.

One day, while walking in the park,
he saw the Virgin Mary in a puddle.

Anselmo wasn't the only survivor
to discover the Virgin,
in a birdbath,
a water fountain,
a rain barrel,
a bucket of sudsy water.

Every sighting accompanied
by the Ave Maria.

CITIZENSHIP

I n 1939, after Hitler invaded Poland, and England and France declared war against Nazi Germany, Carmelo teased his wife, Nina: "Hurry-uppa and be a citizen before the police pick-a you up and send you back-a to Sicily." She waved him away, just like she waved away his pleas to go to night school and learn English. "*Camina* !"—Get out of here! she'd say. "*Non importa* !"—It doesn't matter! Two years later, on December 11, 1941, Germany and Fascist Italy declared war on the United States, and the U.S. Government began to round up Italians as enemy aliens. The next day, Italians were required to surrender hand cameras and radio transmitters. Even "Joltin' Joe" DiMaggio's father, who was a fisherman in the San Francisco Bay Area, had his boat confiscated. Nina and her sister, Mariuzza, scrambled to get their citizenship papers in order. Carmelo said not to worry; his cousin Frank worked at the office of the U.S. Citizenship and Immigration Services. Nina's youngest daughter, Rosa, worked hard to prepare her mother for the test. Her biggest hurdle was Nina's primitive pronunciation of English. On the day of the exam, the clerk—he was new and super-charged with patriotism—asked her, as part of the U.S. History section of the exam, "What did the Emancipation Proclamation do?" Rosa had prepped Nina for this question. "Freed the niggers," Nina said—she couldn't pronounce "Negroes." The startled clerk asked her the question again. "Freed the niggers," she repeated. The clerk wondered if Nina wasn't guilty of "moral turpitude," a factor that could disqualify her from becoming a U.S. citizen. Luckily, Carmelo's cousin got wind of the situation and convinced the clerk to overlook the poor Sicilian immigrant's innocent mispronunciation. Mariuzza also passed her exams, and the two of them celebrated with an orangeade at a Woolworth's counter on Fordham Road.

PHOTO OF DAD SITTING ON A JEEP

The jeep is without doors or hubcaps. A white star is stenciled on the roof, along with the U.S. Army ordinance numbers: 2079495. A spare tire juts out from the rear. Dad sits on the doorframe of the passenger side. His left boot rests on a running board, right foot on the ground. He wears baggy pants and a hooded sweater. A ring gleams from his right hand, a pair of goggles perch like praying mantis eyes on top of his head. His eyebrows are thick and dark, and a smile brightens his face. He looks protean and brash.

The first time Mom's Sicilian-born father—my grandpa—met him, Dad looked so skinny and pale that Grandpa asked Mom, "*Che cos'ha? È malato?*"—What's wrong with him? Is he sick? After six months in the army, he came back on leave with a glowing tan, arms and chest rippling with muscles.

Free for the first time, he's no longer in the shadow of his father, no longer responsible for the physical upkeep of his house, or for keeping his mother happy. Maybe the photo was taken before she threw herself out the window and landed in a mental hospital for three months.

Dad grew bored with his cavalry unit and signed a list to be transferred. But when he learned that the signees were headed for the frontlines, he scratched his name off—some would call it cowardice—but at the war's end, he returned with all four limbs intact.

Grandpa was lenient with his three daughters. He let them go to dances, the roller-skating rink, and bought them cigarettes at the duty-free commissary in the Veterans Hospital where he worked. He even allowed Mom to visit Dad twice in California before they got married. I bet they were getting it on.

CARMELA'S VOICE: *I thought it was normal*

to go to the graveyard every Sunday
with a shopping cart loaded with orchids,
bread, salami, ricotta, roasted peppers,
apricots, sautéed escarole, pears, figs,
biscotti, and my favorite dolls and toys.

While I played and ate, Nonna
joked with her son-in-law, Uncle
Enzo, who never stopped teasing her
about using onions instead of tomato
paste when making her holiday sauce.
She argued with her brother, Uncle Vito,
about who was the rightful owner
of a stone house in a cactus patch
in Sicily, while I played with girls
living behind the family tombstones.

Nonna pleaded with Cousin Giulia
to forgive her son once and for all
for leaving the seminary in Scarsdale
to marry into a family of Calabrese
ice vendors and ditch diggers.

And she begged Nonno Luigi
to forget that Cousin Giuseppe
didn't invite him to his son
Angelo's Confirmation; after all,
wasn't it time to rest in peace?

Nonna sipped her strong black coffee
—she called it jet fuel—greeted
her sisters, Zia Rosa and Zia Maria,
talking in her loud Messinese dialect,
doling out the spiciest gossip,

talking until the sun went down
and the groundskeepers kicked us out.

V-GIRLS, 1944

They loved to skate
with GIs at Gay Blades

share a drink at Childs.
Some traded

bodies for favors
when the rent was due.

THE ITALIANS OF VILLA AVENUE

said their fathers slaved all day
digging tunnels for New York's subway,
then hustled to the Jerome Park Quarry
to lug wheelbarrows filled with
granite blocks to the Grand Concourse
to build Saint Philip Neri Church.

After their back-breaking work,
the shamrock priests took control
of their stone temple, mocked
their broken English, swaggered
at their *feste* like big-bellied lords,
branding them *pagans* for pinning
dollar bills to hand-carved statues
to Santa Assunta and San Antonio.

THE HEARTH

Sparrows screech at sunset
in a Bronx courtyard.

Grandma gives me honey
when I can't stop coughing.

Sunrise means Grandpa's
wink and silver eggcup.

TRADITIONS

To R.C.

Through a mist of steam
from the spaghetti Maria's draining in the sink
her mother-in-law points a gnarled finger at her.
"You broke a tradition," she says.
"What tradition?" Maria asks,
vapors fogging her glasses.
"You didn't name your children after their grandparents."

Maria lowers her head and waits until she leaves the kitchen.
Holding back a smile, she thinks about her sister-in-law's
kids. Marzio whined all through grade school
that the kids called him "Martian,"
demanding that he *take them to his leader*,
while Ninfa fumed that in high school
all the boys called her "Nympho."

VEAL CUTLETS

Villa Avenue, 1950s

Grandma made no bones about it: I was her favorite. She was forever pinching my cheeks and playfully calling me *"Faccia Brutta"*—Ugly Face. As a kid, I loved to go food shopping with her, especially to the butcher shop. She always waited until the butcher served all his other customers, as she demanded extra attention. He'd smile and say, *"Quante libbre, Signora?"*—How many pounds, madam? And, shaking her finger as if she were putting him on notice that *"Non c'è nessuna fessa qui"*—There are no idiots here—she'd say, *"Tre e falle molto sottili!"*—Three, and make them real thin! The butcher would laugh. *"Sempre la stessa storia con Lei"*—Always the same story with you. Then he'd carve cutlets from a thick slab of veal, and using the side of his heavy meat cleaver, he'd start pounding on them. He'd pound and pound and pound. I would stare as he swung at the tender pink meat, his white coat stained with blood, the sound of his cleaver half-slap, half-whack. After each cutlet was thin enough to see through, he'd wrap it in a piece of glossy white paper. At home, Grandma coated the cutlets with egg, bread crumbs, and parsley, and fried them in olive oil. Somehow I'd always slip into the kitchen before anyone else, where Grandma would pinch my cheek and reward *Faccia Brutta* with a golden-brown cutlet.

SISTERS

"Hey, is it raining?"
"How should I know? Stick your finger out the window."
"Don't be fresh; it looks dark."
"It could just be cloudy."
"You think it's gonna come down?"
"Do I look like the Weather Lady?"
"What does the radio say?"
 "Possibility of showers."
"They always say that."
"What do you want from me?"
"Maybe if I bring a small umby, it'll act like a cross."
 "How's that?"
"It'll keep away the rain like a cross keeps away the vampires."
"Why don't you take a wooden stake and hammer while you're at it."

GOOD-BYE BRONX

with your hissing
steam pipes, alley cats,
stickball games,
fig trees in cement.
We're off
to the open spaces
of Springdale, Connecticut.

Behind the wheel
of the bullet-nosed Studebaker,
Dad grins,
Mom dabs tears,
I wave at the old dust mop
shaking out the tenement window.

ADDIO BRONX*

con i tuoi tubi a vapore
che fischiano,
partite di palla e mazza,
fichi nel cemento.
Siamo diretti
verso gli spazi aperti
di Springdale, nel Connecticut.

Al volante
della Studebaker Champion
dal naso a pallottola,
papà fa un largo sorriso
mamma si asciuga le lacrime,
io saluto con la mano,
la scopa a filacce
che si scrolla dalla finestra della palazzina.

---

*   Translated from English into Italian by Professor Luigi Bonaffini

SONS OF RICHES

NATURAL HISTORY

An end-of-the-year school trip from suburban Connecticut
to the New York Museum of Natural History, 1955.

Our bus passes through Harlem: shadows behind sooty
windows, mangy dogs, a ripped mattress on a mountain
of rubble. At 125th Street, Miss Wilson whispers:

*Don't look at the colored people. Last year they threw bricks
and overturned a school bus when white kids stared at them.*

Inside the museum, a bronze African woman's bust, two
naked breasts, polished brightly by a thousand schoolboy hands.

KNEECAPPED

Springdale, Connecticut, 1955

When I trip on the sidewalk along Hope Street,
my knee goes down like an anchor
into the ridges of a foot-high stone wall.

A woman, wrinkled as my grandmother, stops.
I figure she'll comfort me like my Nonna Nina
with her pillowy breasts and buttery pastina soup.

Instead, her blue eyes twinkle as she bends low
to stare more fully into my eyes, streaming tears.
She grins bearishly as I groan, rubs her hands

together while I limp along. A devil of a woman,
wrinkled as my grandmother, wearing a straw derby
with clustered cloth roses.

REBEL RUMBLINGS

To Chuck Berry, 1926-2017

I was a chronic bed-wetter. My teachers mangled
my name, called me *Fag-ee-annie*, no matter how
many times I corrected them. I wore orthopedic
shoes and had stomach cramps in class. I couldn't
sit still and Miss Harrison tied me to my seat with
jump rope. When I couldn't recite my homework,
Miss Wilson shook me, leaving nail prints in my arms.

Then I learned how to turn on Chuck Berry
in my head. His voice jolted me out of my stupor,
his guitar chords, like a tommy-gun, riddled
the blackboard, the bookshelves, the display
cases with prize-winning science projects,
the Stars and Stripes, the Pledge of Allegiance,
the portrait of President Dwight D. Eisenhower.

ODE TO ARMANDO

Springdale Elementary School, 1955

Coarse curly hair with a golden guinea tan,
you showed up with collar up and cuffs down
in front of school, first week of fifth grade

in the days of lead sled Mercurys and low-slung
Harleys with ape-hanger handlebars, "*Mambo Italiano*"
on the juke, *Blackboard Jungle* on the screen.

From your back pocket you pulled a switchblade,
your fingernail pink as you pushed the button,
ten inches of wavy steel flashing in the morning sun.

The girls lollylooped their eyes.
The boys scattered like buckshot.

Armando, King of the Squirts, ahead of your time;
we've missed you.

SONS OF RICHES

T wo of my fifth-grade favorites are Mike, whose father is a bigwig in the telecommunications field, and Whitey, whose dad belongs to the Swedish Diplomatic Corps. They live in mansions set back from Newfield Avenue, an oak-shaded road less than half a mile from our humble Cape Cod. At Mike's place I meet his sister Lacey, a cute blonde with a ponytail, who invites me into the backyard for a game of badminton. She hands me a racket, then disappears into the house at her mother's insistence. Her mother is a lanky woman who looks dressed for a wedding. After grilling me about where I live and what my father does, she tells me I can stay for the afternoon, but not to think about returning, since my family isn't part of their community. I fare worse at Whitey's house, where he and Mike jimmy the door open to the cabin next to the duck pond, and pass out Dunhill cigarettes and glasses of Chivas Regal. High on scotch, Whitey fires a steel-tipped arrow from his dad's hunting bow into a pet swan's ass. That night, his father calls mine and blames me for being a bad influence on his son, forbidding me from ever setting foot on his property again.

WHY I CUT DAD'S HEAD OFF

I find a trunk of photos
in a dusty storage room
below Mom's condo,
snapshots of three generations
celebrating marriages,
graduations, holiday dinners,
Mom in her first bloom of beauty,
Dad in his army uniform,
Sis petting our dog, Dickie.

Pictures, pictures, I flip through them
like playing cards, until I stumble
on a photo of me in Confirmation robes
with my untameable cowlick.
I'm shoulder to shoulder with a man
in an elegant suit, a handkerchief
sprouting from his left pocket. But
someone has taken a scissor and cut
out a square where his head should be.

Then I recall, 1958, I was thirteen,
the year Dad joined a group
of vigilantes who shut down
the State Theater, to drive out of town
what they claimed was an infestation
of over-sexed teenage toughs.

Gone was the 25-cent Saturday afternoon
Kiddie Matinee, the Sunday 50-cent
double-feature, the six-cent candy bars,
the endless stream of cartoons, serials, shorts,
black-and-white and Technicolor movies.

Gone was my oasis of fantasy where I met
Tobor—*robot* spelled backwards—
The Great, shuddered at *The Beast from
20,000 Fathoms, Attack of the 50 Ft
Woman, The Thing*, fell in love
with Judy Garland in *The Wizard of Oz*,
Kim Novak in *Picnic*, and Julie Adams
in *Creature from the Black Lagoon*.

How I hated Dad's guts
for closing down my dream palace
just because a few seats were slashed,
the screen a little pitted from flying objects,
a feel copped here and there in the back rows.
To this day I can't forgive him.
A smile curls my lips, like the yellowing photo
of my beheaded father.

ANGLING

I stuff a tangle
of treble hooks
into a tackle box,
strap on a scaling knife.

Tell myself life
is a largemouth
leaping at flies
on a sleepy afternoon.

Try to forget the back seat
of a pink Pontiac, smell
of saltwater and suntan lotion
on her beach-brown body.

My reel whines, steel-edged bait
plunks into a pond filled with seaweed.

"*MIO AMORE*," BY THE FLAMINGOS

A bank of golden snowflakes
Sunflowers swaying to church bells

The tart bite of early raspberries
A fox flashes among corn stalks

Wheat sprigs caress bare thighs
The smell of simmering marinara sauce

RACE

Dolan Junior High School, 1960

I'd never been much of an athlete, and Coach Pinto,
who'd been held back twice in his senior year
of high school to remain star quarterback, kept
his arms folded, eyes buried in the cinder track.

We were behind by a few yards when the baton
passed to me at the 200-meter line. I gained ground,
rounding the bend side by side with my rival,
a sinewy Negro with long legs and marcelled hair.

I thought about Mom, civil rights advocate, who
had faced down the neighbors, furious at her
for endangering property values by letting Jackie
Robinson's daughter attend my sister's birthday party.

I winced when my opponent rammed his elbow
into my ribs, less from the pain than the shock
of his dark skin touching mine. He elbowed me
again, my adrenaline soared, and I pulled ahead.

When I crossed the finish line, the coach's fists
pumped the air. In the locker room, I forgot about
Mom's lectures about desegregation and social justice,
and cursed black bullies who didn't play by the rules.

GREASER: A NIGHTMARE

Connecticut, 1962

With copious amounts of Wildroot Cream Oil, I comb my curly black hair into a pompadour that tumbles over my forehead like an oily waterfall. Acne constitutes one of the three curses of my teens, and my pomp covers the zits sprouting just below my hairline. Curse number two are the clunky orthopedic Oxfords my parents force me to wear because of my fallen arches. Finally, there is the biggest curse of all: my parents' snub-nosed Nash Rambler. Unlike my buddies, who drive their parents' spiffy, high-performance Pontiacs and Chevys, I'm stuck puttering around with a blue-beaked, six-cylinder shit-box. My bad attitude shows, and in one month alone I dent the trunk, crack both side windows, and lose two hubcaps. This prompts my father to say, "One more mishap and you're grounded." And to be seventeen in Springdale, Connecticut, without a car is to strangle from social asphyxiation.

One Friday morning I slap on a handful of hair tonic and go to my high school English class. A bottle-blonde with ear-to-ear eyebrows and raccoon eyeliner turns around and says, "Jeez, what happened to yer hair; it looks like wet licorice!"

Upset by her remark, I don't sleep well that night, and waking up with a sour stomach, I slather on some Wildroot, tumble my pomp, and go out the door without eating breakfast.

My father lets me use the shit-box, and I plan on visiting a friend who owns a coral-pink 1958 Impala, so I can sit next to him and cruise the streets of Stamford in style. I pull out of the driveway onto Prudence Drive and speed toward Hope Street, where I have to make a sharp turn. As I wait at the stop sign, my mind plays back the blonde's words about my hair, and I feel hoodwinked by my aunts, who go on about my gorgeous locks. Flooring the gas pedal, I jerk onto Hope Street, but my hands—still greasy with Wildroot—can't grip the steering wheel, and it slides through my fingers. I never see the station wagon that hits me head-on, totaling the Rambler, leaving strands of my hair in the cracks of the windshield.

SEEDS

WAR FEVER

Pennsylvania Military College, 1963

I coldcock him in the mouth,
send his choppers flying,
stomp his chest until black bile
bubbles out of his ears and nostrils.
No, I don't do this. But I want to,
one morning, after an upperclassman,
in front of a crowd of students,
twists my name into female genitalia,
calls my mom a floozy, restricts me
to my room for a week, all because
he doesn't like the curvature
of my lower lip when I chant,
"Sir, good morning, Sir!"

NIGHT OF THE HOT HOAGIE

Every night, chest out, face shiny,
Brigade Sergeant Samuel L. Silverman
bursts into my room
10 p.m., hunger hour,
while I stand eyes forward,
gut in, shoulders back,
quivering like I have palsy.
Sergeant Silverman sniffs around
for a Philly-style hoagie sandwich:
cheesesteak, shrimp salad,
hamburger, Italian.

He opens drawers,
looks in coat pockets,
lifts up blankets and sheets,
and when he finds a hoagie,
confiscates half, declaring "R.H.I.P"
—Rank Has Its Privileges—
as the big knot in his throat
works itself up and down,
and half my precious sandwich
disappears down his gullet.

Fed up with being ripped off,
I order an Italian flame-thrower
from Fran and Nan's Hoagie Shop:
prosciutto, salami, and provolone,
all three layers larded with Tabasco,
Louisiana Hot Sauce,
and cherry peppers.

The next evening, Sergeant Silverman
bursts into my room,
picking up the scent of hoagie.

I make no attempt to hide its location.
After the first few bites, Sarge roars
and runs off to the latrine,
where he latches his lips around
the cold water faucet.

GOLD TEETH

Pennsylvania Military College, 1964

Tall and slim in his cadet uniform, with a swarthy, pock-marked face, Silvio never fails to work into his conversation two facts: that his father is rich and that his fiancée is a model. Owner of a lucrative dental practice, and a fastidious dresser, his father often tells his son that while gold teeth were once the hallmark of aristocrats, today you only find them in the mouths of colored people. Silvio's girlfriend, a runner-up for Miss New Jersey, gives him a certain power among his classmates. He lets us know that his fiancée's friends are all models, and that he can—if he's so inclined—fix us up with one of them.

One evening, he introduces me to a blonde named Sandy, who is so taken with my zany wit—enhanced by a heavy indulgence of cheap wine—that she invites me to an upcoming debutante's ball. Images of her shapely body undulating under mine keep me awake at night. The week before the ball, Silvio and I go to a sorority mixer at Glassboro State Teachers College, where I wave at two black girls walking toward us whom I'd met at a previous mixer. Silvio suddenly stops and ducks into the men's room, and after a moment's hesitation, I join him.

Inside, I'm unable to find him at first until, lifting my eyes toward the ceiling, I see him crouched like a gray-legged stork on a ledge above the urinal, opening a window. "I can't be seen with those girls," Silvio hisses, just before he jumps. "Suppose it gets back to my father. And I'm going to make sure Sandy knows you're into black chicks." I close the door and hurry down the hallway, knowing that if I don't catch Silvio in the parking lot, I'll have to thumb a ride back to campus.

SEEDS

Pennsylvania Military College, 1967

I find a recipe in an anarchist magazine
on how to hallucinate using household products,
buy twelve packets of morning glory seeds:
six of Heavenly Blues and six of Pearly Gates.
The salesman asks what a cadet wants with flower seeds.
I tell him I'm the Commandant's aide-de-camp
and they're for his garden.

A chemistry major grinds the seeds
and I pack the powder into triple-X gelatin capsules.
My buddies laugh at me at the Sun City Bar
when I flash my stash of hallucinogens,
but join me in washing the caps down
with 15-cent drafts of Pabst Blue Ribbon.

An hour later at the Friday frat mixer,
I see a cadet walking across a row of chairs
arms out, another stumbling into the band
as the drummer solos on "Wipe Out,"
and a third on his knees, clinging
to the legs of a Haverford sorority sister.

"LOUIE, LOUIE," BY THE KINGSMEN

Spotlight illuminates
rats' eyes in alleyway

Electric eels crack
aquarium glass

G-men shake maracas
filled with fishhooks

CUTTING THE RUG IN PHILLY

When I was young, my father told me that Negroes were born with a natural sense of rhythm, and this explained why they were the undisputed kings and queens of the dance floor. Especially when it came to jazz and rock, the best that whites could do was a mere pale and clumsy imitation of what colored people did so easily. And, indeed, the dancing I saw growing up in Springdale, Connecticut, confirmed my father's notion of Negro dance superiority. Then, in 1964, while a cadet at Pennsylvania Military College, I began to go to dances and clubs in the Philadelphia area. There, to my astonishment, I saw white people doing the Twist, the Fly, the Stomp, the Watusi, the Madison, the Hully Gully, the Pony, and the Mashed Potato, with the same technical skill, the same ease, and the same depth of feeling as their black counterparts. These "whiteys" swayed in big boss lines, shook and shimmied, bopped and boogied—an intrepid few even did splits, handsprings, and knee drops. I'm still grateful to Philly's hip white dancers, who did so much to demolish racial stereotypes.

CAUCASIAN COOL

A CALZONE IN JEFFERSON PARK

115th Street and Pleasant Avenue

Juan pitches, Daryl bats,
Vinnie fields.
"Hey, it's my turn to be up!
I wanna pitch!
Somebody else shag the ball!"

At the water fountain
Daryl barrels in with his big chest
takes the first sip.

Under the plane trees
Juan shows his Indian chief ring
ruby eyes, full headdress.
"In a fist fight
I'd leave feather prints
on your face."

A woman's voice shouts, "Vinnie!"
A man pushing a handcart hollers:
"Pretzels! Ices!" Vinnie runs across the street
into a beat-up brownstone.
Daryl and Juan head for the cart.

Vinnie returns with a turnover
of baked pizza dough
fatter than his forearm,
ricotta, onions, tomato sauce
bubbling up from where he's bitten.
"Hey, what's that?" Daryl and Juan ask.
Vinnie does a little war dance,
pretzel wrappers hit the ground.

DOÑA CARMEN DREAMS OF SAN VITO

I t won't be long now before I meet my Maker. Still, I'm happy to look at the candle flickering on my night table. My daughters think I lit it for Saint Lazarus; they don't know my secret—I burn it for my congressman, Vito Marcantonio, my San Vito. No one, not even my husband, Santos—a good man who died too young—helped me the way Vito did. After Santos died, the Parks Department tried to deny me Santos' pension. Vito cut through the red tape and made sure I got it. And when I couldn't pay the rent, and the marshals put my furniture on the sidewalk, Vito came with men to put my furniture back, and organized a rent party so I had money to give the landlord. And how many times did Vito reach into his own pockets so my kids could have a bite to eat? Most of all, I thank him for saving my son, Carlito, when Italians threatened to kill him for raping one of their sisters. The truth is, this "sister" had a crush on Carlito! With Vito's help, we smuggled my son on a plane wearing a woman's wig so he could hide out in Puerto Rico until Vito straightened things out in New York. If there was any justice in this world, San Vito would have worn the cardinal's robes, and not that hypocrite Spellman.

JUNKIES' PARADISE, 1966

T hat summer I worked in a children's day camp on East 104th Street, between Lexington and Park Avenues, where two herds of *tecatos*—junkies—gamboled like wild horses. Locals referred to the block as "Junkies' Paradise." Every weekday afternoon, a Bonneville ragtop with Jersey plates came down the block and parked in front of a Pentecostal church. Above a dashboard-Madonna hung a pair of fuzzy green, white, and red dice. The driver was short and wore a tan fedora, while his partner was over six feet tall and sported a ponytail. Papo, a neighborhood dealer, joined them inside the car, and after transacting business, would leave, pursued by a pack of *tecatos*. On the last day of the camp, Ponytail stood on the sidewalk arguing with some *tecatos*, when a rock bounced off his head and a fist slammed into his gut. The six-footer fell under a fury of punches, stomps, and stick-blows. I shoved the kids into a doorway, and just as I was about to walk out, Papo ran across the street, with a wine bottle in his hand. Winding up like a pitcher, he threw it at a distance of three feet into the prostrate Jerseyite's face. *Tecatos* scattered and a low moaning came from the sidewalk, *Mamma, Mamma . . .*

ITALIAN DOGS!

L efty was my roommate Pat's ex-cellmate in the Big House. He'd just finished a skid bid for possession, and a few days after his release, he gave me my wings—my first skin-pop of dope. One Sunday, he took me to his parents' place on East 97ᵗʰ Street to hit his mom up for a few bucks. "My pop's been drinking all weekend," he said, "so ignore him if he says anything." Hunched over a coffee table, his father sat in a sleeveless tee shirt, nodding in front of two empty fifths of Seagram's 7. Suddenly, he opened his eyes and started babbling to me in Spanish. At the time, I was a Latino look-alike, with curly black hair, a moustache, and what guys in the neighborhood called un chivo—a goatee. "I'm Italian, not Puerto Rican," I said. "¡*Italiano*!" He jumped up. "¡*Perros italianos*!"— Italian dogs! He lunged at me, and Lefty's mother threw herself between us. A chair turned over, and one of the bottles rolled off the table and smashed on the floor. Lefty managed to pull me through the front door. I took off down the block, toward the Park Avenue El, just as the New Haven commuter train sped north above. Over his mother's pleas to calm down, I heard his father "¿*Italiano*? ¡*Puñeta*! ¡*Lo mato*!"—I'll kill that jerk-off!

FACE-LIFT

P at quits dealing for the day, and to reward his peroxide blonde girlfriend, Judy—who swears she's stopped using—offers to take us to Patsy's Restaurant, near the old Italian neighborhood. I've sworn to my girl, Nilsa, that I've quit using too, but before picking her up, I dust my nose holes with a light powdering of pure to keep down the sickness. I've seen Judy trick under the Park Avenue El and she's caught me at all the hottest copping spots. But, around Pat and Nilsa, we keep the doper's code and dummy up. Inside Patsy's, a waiter with a face like a battered soccer ball twitches in his red dinner jacket as black-plum Pat sits next to lemon-headed Judy. Behind the bar there's a guy with a toothpick sticking out of his mouth and a beefy physique that reminds me of the Mafiosi that are rumored to hang out at Patsy's. We could have had a ring-a-ding time; chowed down, swigged wine, listened to Dino and Frankie on the jukebox, if Judy hadn't taken such a big jolt of H, head rising and falling, face dripping eggplant parmigiana. Pat screams: "Stay awake! Goddamn it! Wipe your face! Goddamn it!" I whisper for him to calm down, as the waiter throws his towel on the floor and the bartender unbuttons his sports jacket.

CONFESSIONS

A woman wrapped in a black scarf slips through
the heavy door and looks around for an empty seat.
Rows of bodies remain rigid as tombstones.
The priest stops his sermon, then his words thunder
off the granite block walls of St. Philip Neri Church:
"You dare to come late to the House of the Lord?"
I'm five, sitting next to my mother, frozen with fear.

Decades later, strung out on dope, I go to the Bronx
to hit up my Uncle Calogero for fix money—I tell him
I need to move. Across the street is St. Philip's. On a lark,
I kneel in the confessional. A window slides open. "Bless me,
Father, for I have sinned; I'm lost, sick . . . I want to die!"
"Be brave, my son," says a voice reeking of whiskey.
I stand up, shake my head. "Wait! Jesus will save you!"
the priest pleads, followed by another zephyr of whiskey.

SICK

Schoolyard, 108th Street, 1968

Bug-eyed and pouring sweat, he strides past children playing in the schoolyard and enters the park. There are about 30 blacks and Puerto Ricans, sitting on benches, playing cards, drinking, smoking weed, snorting dope. Eddie Palmieri's "*Azúcar*" is blasting from a portable radio. "Gimme your stash!" the intruder says, pointing a .38 at Nino, one of Pat's steady customers. Everyone freezes. I'm next to Pablo, who's been telling me how he's going to buy methadone wafers so he can detox a week before his wedding. "Yo, Pat, tell 'em I'm awright," Nino says. I survey the crowd. Nobody gives a shit about this Eyetie junkie from Jersey. I've made it a point to keep away from him, not wanting to remind people I'm Italian too. "Yo, my man, this ain't right," Nino says. The stick-up man shouts, "Look, muthafucka, I'm sick," pistol-whipping Nino in the face, sending him tumbling to the asphalt. I look around. Pat has faded into the crowd. My heart races. *Is it turn-on-whitey time? Am I next?* Suddenly, Pablo leaps up and an explosion rings in my ear. I see blood spurt out of his leg. People run out of the park in all directions. Pablo hobbles toward Second Avenue, throwing his pocketknife at the fleeing gunman.

THE ITALIANS ARE COMING !

I'm an in-the-closet wop, squatting in a park in Spanish Harlem watching white boys buy beat dope, and ginzos from Jersey, robbed of their cop money at gunpoint. Blacks and PRs rule the roost here, and passing as a Latino who is boon-coon tight with Pat, a feared and favored black dope-slinger, is my survival game. After Nandy gets slick with two guineas in a coke deal on Pleasant Avenue, shouts ring out: *The Italians are coming! The Italians are coming!* Ricans and soul brothers grab their jackets and radios, reach under wooden benches for their stashes, and hightail it out of the park like fire-scared ponies. I marvel how quickly people have fled, thrill in secret at the fierce rep of my Roman warrior race. I laugh, the scene is hilarious, for once I don't feel uptight or in danger because of who I am. I survey the cement tables, littered with burning cigarettes, joints, half-drunk bottles of Ballantine Ale. I'm taking a hit from a pint of Georgi's vodka, when I notice a black limousine creeping along Second Avenue, bright flashes from the passenger-side window, pinging sounds all around me. I eat the paving stones, crawl under a cement table, my hands pawing dog shit, tin foil, glass shards.

CAUCASIAN COOL

My ex-roommate Pat had a way
of rolling the vowels of my last name
while lowering his voice,
suggesting my connection
to the Gambino, Genovese,
or other blood-and-guts Mafia families.

A drug peddler by profession,
he'd invite customers to our crib,
put out a spread
of bodega-bought salami and cheese,
Italian bread,
olives with pimientos,
pour Gallo's port into plastic glasses.

I'd sit around in a guinea tee,
Madonna medallion 'round my neck,
black hair slicked back,
the bristles of what Pat called
my pussy-tickler moustache
menacing as cactus needles.
I'd barely mouth a word
until we finished the grit
and sampled Pat's products.
Then I was all praise:
the weed tripped me out,
the coke made my eyeballs clatter,
the dope dropped my head
like a dead tulip.

Everything was copacetic
until my heroin habit took over
and I clipped Pat's stash once too often.
When he cut out on me
I lost my protector,
my cover,
the single most powerful force

that enabled me to finesse
the cutthroat dope scene
of El Barrio.

With Pat by my side
I'd been Caucasian cool,
an OK guy,
one of the fellows,
to be left untouched by predators
unless they wanted to face
a fist-blow or bullet.

But when he bailed out,
my Mafia veneer vaporized
and I joined the rest of the junkies
in their money-grubbing games:
borrowing with no intention of paying,
panhandling,
renting my gimmicks for a taste,
downing counterfeit bills,
selling swag and bum bags,
stealing, swindling.

Then the locals peeped my hole card:
a *blanquito* dopefiend
outsider,
with no guardian, no back-up,
and without the *cojones*
to carry a gun.
Then after being bullied,
beat for money, dope, and stolen goods,
sneered and spat at,
I fled El Barrio and begged my way back
to my folks' house
in Vanillaville, Connecticut.

DELICACIES

Logos (Drug Treatment Program), 1970

The staff says it's my turn
to hustle food donations;
the brothers and sisters are hungry.

I head for Bronx's Little Italy,
Arthur Avenue, where Grandpa's
family lived fifty years ago.
People take pity when I say

I'm an ex-dope addict
struggling to stay off the stuff.
I return with caponata, artichokes,
olives, boxes of rigatoni, penne.

The mostly black and Puerto Rican
residents have little taste
for Italian food. I have a field day
feasting on delicacies.

After a few days the merchants
grumble, but the staff says I can't
take "no" for an answer, and growling
stomachs thunder in my head.

I go to Teitel Brothers,
crates stacked like fortress walls,
repeat *we are a non-profit . . .*
they stop me, *We gave once, twice, three times*

now beat it. I persist. Mr. Teitel
wears a coral horn around his neck,
picks up a five-pound can of tomatoes.
Scram or I'll bounce this off your head.

I clear out, head for the Dominican-owned
bodegas; they give milk, bread, eggs,
potatoes; *Vayas con Dios.*

THE FEAST

Nine months in Logos,
I'm at the San Gennaro Feast
with my girl, Nilsa,
Cousin Dom, his wife, Carmen,
squeezing past food stands
along Mulberry Street,
where my grandparents lived
and my father was born.

Yesterday my roommate
split the program,
refusing to wear a dress
as part of a learning experience
for bad-mouthing the staff.

But today I'm high
on rippling accordion glissandos,
greetings exchanged in *Siciliano,*
Pugliese, Calabrese,
air spicy with peppers and onions,
zeppoles sizzling
in three-foot vats of cooking oil.

Knowing later they will chip in
for my dinner tab,
I say *no thanks*
when Nilsa and Carmen
offer me money
for games of chance
or to pin a dollar on San Gennaro.

We eat at Puglia's,
where a fiftyish woman

in a black dress with a gold medallion
between beach-ball breasts
belts out Neapolitan standards:
"Torna a Surriento," "Malafemmena."
My eyes moisten as I eat my antipasto.

I look at my cousin,
married, working, with a college diploma,
while I'm mired in memories:
face slammed into a wall by narcos,
birthday in a mental hospital,
bloody body carried down from a rooftop.

Still, I'm happy today; it's just
the singer's every note grabs me in the gut
and now the tears are flowing.
Dom half-covers his face with his napkin.
I excuse myself, hustle off to the bathroom.
When I return, the music has stopped.
Soon I'll start school,
find a job, move in with Nilsa.

THE MISSING MADONNA

MOURNING MAN

I long for a past
that never was

but will always be
stuck

in a state
of permanent bereavement.

I DREAM I TALK ITALIAN WITH GRANDMA

She looks like she always looked,
stooped over, a few strands
of wiry hair on her head,
brown moles staining her face,
her mood sad, resigned.
Come stai? I ask.

She smiles, reaches out,
squeezes my cheek.
Vorrei parlare Italiano con te—
I'd like to talk Italian with you,
I say, having taken Italian classes
for years preparing for this moment.
Ma che dici?—but
what are you saying?
she answers.

I think, perhaps she can't
speak the language of Dante
but only her native dialect.
Puoi capirmi—can you understand me?
I say half-heartedly.
She squeezes my cheek again.
Si, certo, Gilberto, tu parli bene—
yes, sure, you speak well, Gilbert.

I ask if she ever misses her family
in Italy. *Sure*, she says, *but not like
before. I used to complain so much,
one day your grandfather yelled,
that's it, let's pack up and go back.
But by then it was too late; your mother
and her sisters had roots in America.
It wouldn't have been fair to them.*

I tell her I've visited her hometown,
and confirm what she always claimed
—the lemons are as big as grapefruits.

She tells me about her sister Angela,
her brother Attilio, how it was growing up,
the six Aeolian Islands in full view
from her bedroom window.

As she talks, the moles and wrinkles fade,
she stands upright, a rhythmic motion
in her hips, chestnut hair bouncing,
her hands dancing with every word.

SACRED SOD

Blowing a fly
from his olive-stained thumb
five-foot-two Tito
rises from the table
as his daughter Enza
feeds her uneaten dinner
to the cats flocking
in front of the doorway.

He slips past the purple
pop-bead curtain
that leads to his bedroom,
fumbles for his keys
among the framed photos
of *il Duce*,
and glancing
at Enza's tear-streaked face,
walks to the hilltop cemetery
where his ancestors are buried.

It's his third visit of the day.

Beyond the rusty gate
the air is heavy with basil,
rosemary, and the ear-drilling
drone of cicadas.

White Calabrian sunlight
coats branches sagging with
nugget sacks of figs and pears
and tomatoes burst
like bloody wounds.

Squeezed for space,
Tito trips over a zucchini,
big as a boa constrictor,
and remembers his vow
to bring to court
the five *paesani* who
share his cemetery garden
for encroaching
on his family's sacred sod.

At the tombstones
of his mother and father
he stops to whisper that
his other daughters
have said that Enza is crazy;
feeding her cats that multiply
with every passing day,
never leaving the house;
her skin like *scamorza*
that no man would want to touch.
She needs to see
a head doctor, they tell him.

Tito watches a rabbit nibble
a fallen beanstalk
and ruminates about his
wayward daughters
who have abandoned
the family hearth
for strange blood,
simpy husbands
who buy them fancy dresses
for fancy jobs,
who plead instead of lead.

He is right,
the underground voices
reassure him.
Enza is safe at home;
safe and rooted.

HOLDOUT

The Bronx, 1974

S tricken with osteoporosis, Nina walks like she's shouldering a 50-pound sandbag. Her doctor says it won't be long before she's wheelchair-bound. Her daughter, Rosa, begs her to move to Yonkers with her and her husband, but Nina refuses, saying that in-laws are the scourge of a happy marriage. Years ago, Nina's tenement sang in *Napoletano, Calabrese, Siciliano*. Today, high-decibel Spanish, slapping dominoes, and conga drums dominate her soundscape. Nina comments to Rosa about the odor of onion that wafts through her building. "Mamma, that's not onion," Rosa says. "That's marijuana! Junkies live next door!" One night, Nina sits on her bed, praying to Saint Anthony, when the ceiling collapses. Chunks of plaster shear her cheekbone, break her nose, and knock her unconscious. The neighbors rush her to Fordham Hospital. When Rosa arrives, she sees winos in the waiting room, and demands that her mother be transferred to a Catholic hospital. Rosa's husband hires a lawyer from his Knights of Columbus Lodge to sue Nina's landlord, who had promised for months to fix a water leak in her ceiling but never got around to making the repairs. The lawyer pleads with Nina to testify at the courtroom proceedings, but she shakes her head. "I no wanna make-a no trouble." Not long after, Nina insists on moving to the Blackrock Nursing Home—despite her children's protests. When Rosa brings her a $5,000 settlement check for damages, Nina says it's too much money, but thanks Saint Anthony for giving her a gift to leave her grandchildren.

POE PARK, THE BRONX

And so being young and dipped in folly
I fell in love with melancholy.
—Edgar Allan Poe

S ummertime, early '50s, Grandpa Carmelo takes my hand and brings me to the giant gazebo with ten columns and verdigris crown in Poe Park, where a band wearing maroon uniforms plays Strauss waltzes and dancers twirl and glide from side to side. Frankfurters, cigar smoke, and pomade perfume the evening air while I laugh at the occasional winks of fireflies.

I return to the arson-plagued Bronx, where in the mid-'80s teenage boys hawk *jumbo crack*, living for ten years in the building where Mom's best friend resided when it had a liveried doorman, and across the street, St. James Park boasted one of the best clay tennis courts in New York City.

Around the corner, at the Poe Cozy Nook, Dad took Mom for a drink after a date, long before it became a hot spot for prostitution. Once, while playing with my six-year-old son Mario in Poe Park, a drunken man fired a pistol in the air. People screamed, and I grabbed my son and dove to the ground.

Getting up, I saw, across the Grand Concourse, the faded elegance of the Knights of Columbus Lodge my father—Mario Senior—swore blackballed him because he was Italian.

CURSE OF ELLIS ISLAND

For Maria Bomba Fagiani

I wanted to visit my father's family in Abruzzo, but his first cousin refused to give me their address. She said our relatives hated my grandfather Comincio because he wouldn't help support his mother, who died in rags. As his grandson, I wasn't welcome there. My great-grandmother Maria's husband and children, including my grandfather and his brother Oscar, had jobs in New York. Alone and unable to make ends meet, Maria sold her possessions and abandoned her home in Abruzzo to join her family. Arriving at Ellis Island, she was quarantined for weeks because of an eye inflammation, and sent back to Italy. The examining doctors said her eye ailment might be contagious, and they couldn't risk her infecting Americans. It was the third time she had made it to Ellis Island, and the third time she was repatriated. Who would pay Maria's expenses in Italy? This question led to fighting between her sons. Comincio said the money he wired served as her lifeline. Oscar visited her every year in Abruzzo, brought her gifts, paid for everything, he claimed, including her burial expenses after she was killed during an American bombing raid as the German Army retreated.

SIZE IN SICILY

Sicilians say
everything in America is bigger:
buildings, streets
bars, cars
food portions
even people's backsides.
But in an outdoor market
in the 10,000 *abitanti* town
of Capo d'Orlando
there are six-foot zucchinis
yellow peppers the size of footballs
and lemons
—that if they fell on your head—
could cause a concussion.

MISURA IN SICILIA*

Dicono i siciliani che
in America tutto è più grande:
i palazzi, le strade
i bar, le macchine
le porzioni di cibo
addirittura i sederi.
Ma in un mercato all'aperto
nel paesino di 10.000 abitanti chiamato
Capo d'Orlando
si trovano zucchine di due metri
peperoni gialli grandi come palloni
e dei limoni che,
se ti cascassero in testa,
ti farebbero entrare in coma.

---

* Translated from English into Italian by Professor Paul D'Agostino

DAY TRIP IN SICILY

Except for its stately Norman castle, Caccamo is a common-place town, though later we hear it's home to Sicily's most powerful crime families. Before we leave, clouds—the same angry gray as the tent caterpillars' nests blighting the countryside—choke off the sunlight. Within minutes, the sky roars with thunder, and lightning flashes emblazon the sky. It hasn't rained in months, and the sun-hardened earth can't absorb the deluge. On the coast road, water cascades from cliffs, sweeping dirt, cacti, and stones past wooden barriers, dumping everything onto the road. We weave past stalled cars, trucks, *motorini*— motor scooters—expecting any moment that the rising water will reach our distributor cap, killing the engine, and leaving us stranded. By the time we reach my mother's hometown of Capo d'Orlando, the downpour has stopped, but our nerves are frazzled.

At *cena*—supper—we tell my cousins about the flooding. They look at us like we have breathed too many exhaust fumes. "*Era niente*"—It was nothing—they say about the storm, when the dining room light sparks and the house goes dark. "*Interruzione!*" somebody hollers. People scramble, pulling out a kerosene lantern from under the kitchen sink. My cousins pump the lantern and light matches but can't ignite the wick. Finally, my wife, who works out at the gym every day, grabs the lantern and pumps it like a basketball. A match is struck. There's an explosion, and my heart freezes in fear that her face, her lovely face that I never tire of gazing at, has been burned. When the power comes on, I rejoice to see her skin unmarked, while my cousins compare, unfavorably, the biscotti we brought from Caccamo to those made around the corner.

STRIPPING

Barletta, Puglia, Italy

While anti-immigrant websites
quote Hitler calling race-mixing
a mortal sin, a Red Cross volunteer,
on his first night of service, looks
into the eyes of a young Afghani
huddled in an abandoned warehouse,
frozen and slick with oil after riding
under a truck for 48 hours from Greece.
The volunteer feels *il cuore scaldare*
dell'indifferenza—his apathetic heart
warm up—and like a man possessed,
strips off his coat, hat, scarf, gloves,
and thermal pants, and hands them
to the shivering refugee.

❭

PEELING AN ORANGE IN PALERMO

Early Monday morning
in the vast dining room of the Albergo San Paolo,
a man with five days' stubble
nurses a *caffè ristretto,*
smokes cigarette after cigarette.

A waiter with cinder-gray eyebrows,
in a starched beige jacket, asks:
Qualcosa di più?
Without moving his red-runny eyes,
the smoker grunts: *Arancia.*

The waiter pivots to a table
piled high with apples, kiwis, pears,
pineapples, tangerines, and bananas,
picks out an orange
and with the prongs of a chrome serving fork
pins it to a silver platter.

With a few strokes of a carving knife
he removes the skin in one long peel,
pulling the blood-ripe pulp
through the waxy-white skin
like a flayed lamb through its fur.

The knife cuts through the air
with the fury of an orchestral baton,
leaving six fillets of *arancia*
glistening on the silver platter,
which the waiter sets
in front of the young man,
whose eyes stay fixed
to the tip of his cigarette.

PUPPETS IN PALERMO

Along the dark street
building walls ooze
moss, water, waste.
I step over dogs
with fly-clotted wounds,
mouths opening soundlessly.

I take a front-row seat
in the puppet theater.
The curtain opens;
pupi clank to center stage.
I notice to the left
a young woman wearing
only a black bra,
her hair bouncing
as she jerks the iron bar
and puppet wires.

The *pupi* bow to the audience:
Carlo Magno, lilies on his armor,
shield, and crown;
Orlando, in blue, squint-eyed,
an eagle on his helmet,
cross on his shield;
Rinaldo, decked out in red,
his armor bearing the sign of the lion.

Arrayed against them
are the Saracens
in their oriental outfits:
brutti, dark, glowering.
Finally, there's Angelica,
in flowing white gown;
it is for her honor that

the Paladins and Sacracens
are locked in mortal combat.

The action picks up,
sounds of clashing swords.
I can't keep my eyes off
the young woman, her breasts
brimming out of cloth cups,
her hips shaking
as she yanks the iron bar,
steel wires,
stomps her feet on the floor.

The battle ends;
Orlando and Rinaldo
slaughter the Saracens,
Angelica's honor is saved.
The puppeteers step out
to audience applause,
the bra-wearing beauty
turns her back.

RUSH HOUR IN PALERMO

L'ora di punta—rush hour.
The street curves
and the sidewalk is under construction.
We walk along a stretch of dark alleyways
where a three-legged dog lunges at me
leaving slaver on my jacket pocket.

I feel the mutt's mucus
while reaching for my handkerchief
after my wife gashes her head
on some angle iron jutting out of a stand
where a *pescatore*
sells slithery sea urchins—*ricci di mare*—
to drivers who dash out of double-parked cars.

SUNSET IN PALERMO

In the flame-flickers of *tramonto*
the American tourists
gather in front of a caved-in building
in the Kalsa section of Palermo
marveling at the neat flower murals
painted on the walls
still standing
fifty years
after being bombed
by American Superfortresses.

TRAMONTO A PALERMO*

Nei tremoli delle fiamme
i turisti americani
si radunano di frente un'edificio crollato
nel quartiere di Kalsa di Palermo
meravigliandosi ai murali ordinati dei fiori
dipinti nei muri
ancora in piedi
cinquanta anni
dopo essere bombarate
da Superfortezze statuitensi.

---

* Translated from English into Italian by Gil Fagiani

ROTTEN ROOTS

Basilicata, Italy

We spent the morning twisting and turning
up mountain roads until we reached San Chirico
Raparo, the town my father's mother's
family emigrated from 100 years ago.

At the *municipio*—the town hall—the clerk
couldn't be bothered looking through birth
records without an exact name and date.

"Di Serio," we pleaded. "The family name is Di Serio."
"That means *niente, niente*"—nothing, nothing!
the clerk hollered. "Half the town has that name;
I'm a Di Serio and you're no relative of mine!"

UNA PAROLA

Finale di Pollina, Sicily

—one word—the old Italian ladies say,
holding up a single finger
as they step in front of you at the bank, post office,
ignoring the half hour, forty-five minutes, hour
you've jockeyed behind the ragged excuse
for a line, always about to hemorrhage
into three or four smaller lines,
inching toward a single window teller.
Una parola becomes a paragraph, page,
and while you slowly burn, the old ladies
are opening their purses, transacting business.
"I have diabetes, gout, heart disease," they say
if your eyes betray your anger.

Old San Juan, Puerto Rico

MY WIFE ASKS A QUESTION, HALF IN ITALIAN, HALF IN SPANISH

The uniformed tourist guide says, "*Italiano,*
io parlo italiano. I just returned from Milano;
I love Italian music: Rossini, Verdi, Puccini."
"Latin music," my wife chimes in, "is great too."
"Latin music moves the body," the guide says.
"Italian music moves the mind." Below the counter
he pulls out a *panettone* he bought at Marshalls.
"That's good with *mantequilla*," my wife says.
"Oh, no," he says. "It should be dunked in coffee,
like the *italiani*." When we mention that our families
are from Calabria and Sicily, he says, "Whoa!"
laughs, shapes his hands into a tommy-gun.
Through clenched teeth I say, "That's not funny."
"Pow, pow, pow, pow, pow, rat-tat-tat," he grins.

ETHIOPIA

Nonna fed me pastina with escarole
bought me ices and slices of focaccia
calmed my cough with spoonfuls of honey.

When she eyed my bandaged head
after Butchie Malizzio hit me with a rock
she shamed my father into making Butchie lay off.

Years later I found out she sent Mussolini
her wedding ring to finance the war machine
that bombed and gassed the Ethiopians into submission.

Povera nonna,
like Christopher Columbus
she's lost her saintly luster.

THE SHEPHERD

The Madonie Mountain Range, Sicily

We hear clunking sounds and my cousin Serena says *caprette*. Goats pour down a grassy slope, waves of horns and hair, big ones, skinny ones, some with teats swollen with milk, others wearing wooden collars, swinging copper bells. They spill onto the road, a steady, clip-clopping beat. An older goat leaps over a guard rail, then another, and another, and another. Swirls of dust, bahs, bleats. The pace picking up, the goats' cries growing louder, more frantic. They squeeze under the iron rail, pile into each other, stagger off after smashing their heads. A lone urchin is stranded in the street, mouth stretched open, bleating. He looks so pitiful I'm tempted to pick him up and carry him to the other side of the road, but I fear butts, bites, ticks—Lyme disease. Fifty yards down the road a harsh gutteral sound. We see a tall, bronzed man flailing at stray goats with a ten-foot bamboo pole, a piece of rawhide on the end. The man has milky azure eyes, scruffy beard, shoulder-length hair parted in the middle. He's young but toothless. My wife says he looks like a feral Moses. "*Buon Giorno*," we mutter, heads down, walking faster, afraid to look him in the face. Staring straight ahead, he grunts and lashes the *caprette*, who slow down, stop bleating, line up one behind the other, ranks flowing smoothly, like a hirsute River Jordan.

CHIANTI IN THE CATSKILLS

Haunted sleep, I seek relief walking the streets of Astoria.
At 28th Street, I run into the glittering profile of the Empire
State Building, where my father worked in an executive suite
in the 1960s. I see him in his businessman's suit, white shirt,
clip-on tie, spit-shined shoes—a legacy of his five years
in the cavalry. He smiles, pumps my hand. "Cheer up, enjoy
the sunny weather, think positive thoughts." Then I remember
the letters I found that he wrote to my mother while vacationing
with his paisans in the Catskills. He mentioned that his own father
had come up to join him and how much his gang loved his dad,
a real live wire, who could pull wine corks with the best of them.
I stop in my tracks. A small flock of pigeons peck at a pizza crust.
I'd never wanted to hang out with my dad when I was a young man.

THE MISSING MADONNA II

Villa Avenue, The Bronx, 1989

They canceled the feast
after eighty-one years.

No more uniformed
marching bands
blaring martial music.

No banners of saints
and martyrs
billowing in the wind.

No trembling hands
touching
the silver Madonna.

Just an urban intersection
rank with exhaust fumes

and a field of weeds
capped with razor wire.

DECAY

Mom's 85, calls this morning, tells me she has an infected molar. The dentist says the tooth has to go. Growing up, I thought of Mom as the neighborhood beauty; no physical flaws, white teeth perfectly formed. She taught me racial equality, to defend the poor, but also schooled me to care for my teeth, which tells a lot, she said, about class and character. During her call, Mom's voice trembles, she doesn't know why she's losing her molar, she sees the dentist every six months and brushes and flosses three times a day.

That night I wake up,
a noose of sweat around my neck,
Ku Klux Klansmen
chiseling the enamel off my teeth,
showing home videos of black women
getting their heads blown off.

AFTER VISITING MOM AT COURTLAND GARDENS SUBACUTE CARE FACILITY

Stamford, Connecticut, 1995

Main Street shrivels into a condom.
I sneeze and find three teeth in my hand.
The train doors crush my wristwatch.
I flush the toilet and the ceiling comes down.
I taste blood sucking on a cough drop.
Taco wrappers snap at my feet.

PAT CASTALDO PLAYGROUND

Villa Avenue, Bronx, 2016

Padlocks, two round and two square, hang
from rusty chains clasping the front gate.
Tree branches weigh down the four walls
of schoolyard fence wire. Inside, buckling
asphalt is pierced by spires of Golden Rod.
The stench of waste and noxious weeds
singes the nostrils. Long shadow shards
cut across a pink stroller without wheels,
paper plates, beer, and soda cans. Spider
webs smudge orange-tipped mop handle,
Newport cigarette boxes, Stick-Em City
mouse traps. Claw-shaped leaves climb
poles to hoopless, basketless backboards.

HOLY WATER

Capo d'Orlando, Sicily, 2015

I 'm floating on my back in the *Mar Tirreno*. Behind me are the misty lumps of the Aeolian Islands. The water is buoyant, and I think of Mom, who died three months ago. She migrated from this azure-lapped town in 1921 because Grandpa couldn't find work, a town where people now believe enough in the future to have children.

Along the beach, a platoon of Bangladeshi men peddle the same wares: baseball caps, batteries, cigarette lighters, sunglasses, and knock-off watches and jewelry, while their wives wash their children in the public showers and stuff diapers into overflowing garbage cans. At night, entire families sleep in the wooden boats banked on the shore.

I see myself climbing 230 stair steps with Mom's cousin Sara, well into her 80s, up to the hilltop chapel of the Madonna of Capo d'Orlando, who is said to have healed children suffering from smallpox and warned the townspeople of the arrival of Turkish pirates. Sara, the matriarch of Mom's family, was born on Lampedusa, a speck of an island, closer to North Africa than Sicily, which has become an entry point into Italy for desperate refugees seeking jobs, safety, and political asylum. Twenty-five thousand people have drowned trying to reach Lampedusa's rocky coast.

Sara graduated from the *Università degli Studi di Palermo* in 1939, when few women went beyond the fourth grade. To the consternation of her colleagues, she married a student 10 years younger than herself. Not long after their marriage, he was stricken with multiple sclerosis and became wheelchair-bound. Some of the townspeople whispered that this was divine punishment for her *superbia*—pride—for not accepting her place.

Sara became everyone's *professoressa*, and after teaching three generations Latin, Greek, Italian, Dante, Petrarch, Boccaccio, and Leopardi—her favorite poet—her vocal chords gave out, making it impossible for her to talk. She died at 92.

Mom died at 95, after languishing from dementia for eight years. In her final month, she started speaking Sicilian, decades after she last spoke it with her mother or her *Orlandini* relatives.

I drift with the tide, and for the first time in years see, in the waves, my mother's smile and her expansive presence, before she shriveled with her illness. I'm at peace with Mom, Sara, and the Madonna of Capo d'Orlando.

POSTSCRIPT

LANGUAGE LESSONS AND MOM

Toward the end of Mom's life, after ten years of suffering from Alzheimer's disease, her live-in aide reported to me that she was lying awake half the night, muttering in Italian. I wasn't surprised. Having worked for 12 years in a Bronx mental hospital, I often encountered patients, in the throes of a mental breakdown, regressing and speaking their first tongues, even though, in some cases, their relatives had rarely—if ever—heard them speak it.

A few months before Mom passed away, while I was visiting her, she started speaking in Sicilian; it was Sicilian, not Italian, that was her first tongue. I was able to make out what she was saying—"*Li cosi nun vannu boni*" ("Things aren't going well")—and I started asking her simple questions in Italian: "*Mamma, come ti senti?*" ("Mamma, how do you feel?") She responded by repeating that things "*nun sunu boni*"—weren't good. It was the first conversation I'd had with her in years.

Then I began to reflect. I'd been taking Italian lessons for over twenty years, first at *Scuola Italiana del Greenwich Village*, next to Our Lady of Pompeii Church—coincidentally, the very first church Mom had attended when she first emigrated from Sicily. Over the years, I'd felt so much frustration at having to struggle to learn Italian. At times I was angry at Mom: Why couldn't she have spoken to me in Italian, or at least in dialect, when I was growing up, and made things easier for me?

But after speaking Italian to Mom, and hearing her respond in her first and most heartfelt language, I realized that all the time and money I had invested, all the frustration I had experienced over the years, had been worth it.

MUSICAL SOURCES

1. "*E Lucevan Le Stelle*," sung by Enrico Caruso, from the opera *Tosca*, by Giacomo Puccini
2. "Nocturne in D-flat major," Frédéric Chopin
3. "Roll Over Beethoven," Chuck Berry
4. "*Mambo Italiano*," Rosemary Clooney
5. "*Mio Amore*," The Flamingos
6. "Wipe Out," The Surfaris
7. "Louie, Louie," The Kingsmen
8. "The Twist," Chubby Checker
9. "The Fly," Chubby Checker
10. "Foot Stompin,'" The Flares
11. "The Wah-Watusi," The Orlons
12. "The Madison Time," Ray Bryant
13. "(Baby) Hully Gully," The Olympics
14. "Pony Time," Chubby Checker
15. "Mashed Potato Time," Dee Dee Sharp
16. "Everybody Loves Somebody," Dean Martin
17. "Come Fly With Me," Frank Sinatra
18. "*Azúcar Pa' Ti*," Eddie Palmieri
19. "*Torna a Surriento*," Sergio Franchi
20. "*Malafemmena*," Jimmy Roselli
21. "The Beautiful Blue Danube," Johann Strauss
22. "*Va, Pensiero*," from the opera *Nabucco*, Giuseppe Verdi
23. "The William Tell Overture," Gioachino Rossini

ACKNOWLEDGMENTS

"Mourning Man," "The Black Hand," *Skidrow Penthouse*, #14, 2011.

"*Testa Rossa*—Redhead," *No Distance Between Us: Italian American Poets of Long Island*, edited by: Robert Savino and James Wagner, Local Gems Press, 2017.

"Bad Bread," "Size in Sicily," *Sweet Lemons: Writings With a Sicilian Accent*, edited by: Venera Fazio and Delia De Santis, Legas, 2004.

"His Feet Are His Mother's," *Philadelphia Poets*, Volume 18, 2012.

"Hunger," "Ethiopia," *Avanti Popolo: Italian American Writers Sail Beyond Columbus*, edited by the Italian-American Political Solidarity Club, Manic D Press, 2008.

"Melting Potty," *Performance Poets Association Annual Literary Journal*, 2010.

"*L'America*," *Writing Our Way Home*, edited by Licia Canton and Caroline Morgan Di Giovanni, Guernica Editions, 2013.

"Aunt Lia," *Association of Italian Canadian Writers, 2014 Conference Anthology*, 2015.

"American Now," *Chianti in Connecticut*, Bordighera Press, 2010.

"I Thought It Was Normal," *Paterson Literary Review*, Issue 43, 2015—2016.

"The Italians of Villa Avenue," *Philadelphia Poets*, Volume 23, 2017.

"Sisters," "War Fever," *Home Planet News Online*, Issue 5, 2017.

"Good-bye Bronx," *Journal of Italian Translation*, Volume VI, Spring—Fall 2011.

"Kneecapped," *Ovunque Siamo*. 2018.

"Rebel Rumblings," *The New Verse News*, April 18, 2017.

"Night of the Hot Hoagie," *Rooks*, Rain Mountain Press, 2007.

"Cutting the Rug in Philly," *Levure littéraire*, 2015.

"Seeds," *The Red Wheelbarrow No. 10*, 2017.

"A Calzone in Jefferson Park," "Photo of Dad Sitting on a Jeep," *Paterson Literary Review, Issue 44*, 2016—17.

"Delicacies," "The Feast," *Logos*, Guernica Editions, 2015.

"I Dream I Talk Italian with Grandma," *Fiele-Festa*, 2013.

 "Sacred Sod," Grandpa's Wine," *Feile-Festa*, Spring 2008.

"Stripping," 2017 *AIPF di-vêrsé-city Anthology*.

"Peeling an Orange in Palermo," "Puppets in Palermo," *Descant* 154, Fall 2011.

"Rush Hour in Palermo," *Philadelphia Poets*, Volume 21, 2015.

"Sunset in Palermo," *Medicinal Purposes: A Literary Review*, Vol. II, No. IX, 2003.

"Rotten Roots," *Philadelphia Poets*, Volume 24. 2018.

"The Missing Madonna," *Italian Heart and Italian Soul*, edited by Edward Albert Maruggi, Winston Publishing, 2004.

"Doña Carmen Dreams of San Vito," *Feile-Festa*, Spring 2014.

"Decay," *Skidrow Penthouse*, Spring 2006.

"The Shepherd," *Italian Americana*. 2018.

"Language Lessons and Mom," City Room Blog (formerly known as Metropolitan Diary), *The New York Times*, June 30, 2015.

ABOUT THE AUTHOR

Gil Fagiani (1945-2018) grew up in Stamford, Connecticut. He was a translator, essayist, short-story writer, and poet. His work has been translated into French, Greek, Italian, and Spanish, and his translations have appeared in such anthologies as *A New Map: The Poetry of Migrant Writers in Italy*, edited by Mia Lecomte and Luigi Bonaffini; *Poets of the Italian Diaspora*, edited by Luigi Bonaffini and Joseph Perricone; and *Italoamericana: The Literature of the Great Migration, 1880—1943*, edited by Francesco Durante and Robert Viscusi (American Edition).

He has published five books of poetry; his most recent is *Logos* (Guernica Editions, 2015), and in addition, has published *Stone Walls*, *Chianti in Connecticut*, *A Blanquito in El Barrio*, and *Rooks*; plus three chapbooks, *Crossing 116th Street*, *Grandpa's Wine*, and *Serfs of Psychiatry*. In 2016, his essay "What Does It Mean to Be White in America: My Multi-Metamorphoses" appeared in *What Does It Mean to Be White In America? Breaking the White Code of Silence, A Collection of Personal Narratives* (2Leaf Press). Most recently, his poem "Miss Johnson is Dead" appeared in *Black Lives Have Always Mattered: A Collection of Essays, Poems, and Personal Narratives* (2Leaf Press).

Fagiani co-curated the Italian American Writers' Association's monthly reading series in Manhattan and co-founded the Vito Marcantonio Forum. He worked for 12 years in a Bronx psychiatric hospital, and directed a residential treatment program for recovering alcoholics and drug addicts in Downtown Brooklyn for 21 years. In February 2014, he was the subject of a *New York Times* article by David Gonzalez, "A Poet Mines Memories of Drug Addiction."

VIA FOLIOS

A refereed book series dedicated to the culture of Italians and Italian Americans.

Bassetti. Vol 55. Italian Studies. $8

GIOSE RIMANELLI. *The Three-legged One.* Vol 54. Fiction. $15

CHARLES KLOPP. *Bele Antiche Stòrie.* Vol 53. Criticism. $25

JOSEPH RICAPITO. *Second Wave.* Vol 52. Poetry. $12

GARY MORMINO. *Italians in Florida.* Vol 51. History. $15

GIANFRANCO ANGELUCCI. *Federico F.* Vol 50. Fiction. $15

ANTHONY VALERIO. *The Little Sailor.* Vol 49. Memoir. $9

ROSS TALARICO. *The Reptilian Interludes.* Vol 48. Poetry. $15

RACHEL GUIDO DE VRIES. *Teeny Tiny Tino's Fishing Story.* Vol 47.
Children's Literature. $6

EMANUEL DI PASQUALE. *Writing Anew.* Vol 46. Poetry. $15

MARIA FAMÀ. *Looking For Cover.* Vol 45. Poetry. $12

ANTHONY VALERIO. *Toni Cade Bambara's One Sicilian Night.* Vol 44.
Poetry. $10

EMANUEL CARNEVALI. *Furnished Rooms.* Vol 43. Poetry. $14

BRENT ADKINS. et al., Ed. *Shifting Borders. Negotiating Places.* Vol 42.
Conference. $18

GEORGE GUIDA. *Low Italian.* Vol 41. Poetry. $11

GARDAPHÈ, GIORDANO, TAMBURRI. *Introducing Italian Americana.* Vol
40. Italian/American Studies. $10

DANIELA GIOSEFFI. *Blood Autumn/Autunno di sangue.* Vol 39. Poetry. $15/$25

FRED MISURELLA. *Lies to Live By.* Vol 38. Stories. $15

STEVEN BELLUSCIO. *Constructing a Bibliography.* Vol 37. Italian
Americana. $15

ANTHONY JULIAN TAMBURRI, Ed. *Italian Cultural Studies 2002.* Vol 36.
Essays. $18

BEA TUSIANI. *con amore.* Vol 35. Memoir. $19

FLAVIA BRIZIO-SKOV, Ed. *Reconstructing Societies in the Aftermath of War.*
Vol 34. History. $30

TAMBURRI. et al., Eds. *Italian Cultural Studies 2001.* Vol 33. Essays. $18

ELIZABETH G. MESSINA, Ed. *In Our Own Voices.* Vol 32. Italian/
American Studies. $25

STANISLAO G. PUGLIESE. *Desperate Inscriptions.* Vol 31. History. $12

HOSTERT & TAMBURRI, Eds. *Screening Ethnicity.* Vol 30. Italian/
American Culture. $25

G. PARATI & B. LAWTON, Eds. *Italian Cultural Studies.* Vol 29. Essays. $18

HELEN BAROLINI. *More Italian Hours.* Vol 28. Fiction. $16

FRANCO NASI, Ed. *Intorno alla Via Emilia.* Vol 27. Culture. $16

ARTHUR L. CLEMENTS. *The Book of Madness & Love.* Vol 26. Poetry. $10

JOHN CASEY, et al. *Imagining Humanity.* Vol 25. Interdisciplinary Studies. $18

ROBERT LIMA. *Sardinia/Sardegna.* Vol 24. Poetry. $10

DANIELA GIOSEFFI. *Going On.* Vol 23. Poetry. $10

ROSS TALARICO. *The Journey Home.* Vol 22. Poetry. $12

EMANUEL DI PASQUALE. *The Silver Lake Love Poems*. Vol 21. Poetry. $7

JOSEPH TUSIANI. *Ethnicity*. Vol 20. Poetry. $12

JENNIFER LAGIER. *Second Class Citizen*. Vol 19. Poetry. $8

FELIX STEFANILE. *The Country of Absence*. Vol 18. Poetry. $9

PHILIP CANNISTRARO. *Blackshirts*. Vol 17. History. $12

LUIGI RUSTICHELLI, Ed. *Seminario sul racconto*. Vol 16. Narrative. $10

LEWIS TURCO. *Shaking the Family Tree*. Vol 15. Memoirs. $9

LUIGI RUSTICHELLI, Ed. *Seminario sulla drammaturgia*. Vol 14. Theater/ Essays. $10

FRED GARDAPHÈ. *Moustache Pete is Dead! Long Live Moustache Pete!*. Vol 13. Oral Literature. $10

JONE GAILLARD CORSI. *Il libretto d'autore. 1860 – 1930*. Vol 12. Criticism. $17

HELEN BAROLINI. *Chiaroscuro: Essays of Identity*. Vol 11. Essays. $15

PICARAZZI & FEINSTEIN, Eds. *An African Harlequin in Milan*. Vol 10. Theater/Essays. $15

JOSEPH RICAPITO. *Florentine Streets & Other Poems*. Vol 9. Poetry. $9

FRED MISURELLA. *Short Time*. Vol 8. Novella. $7

NED CONDINI. *Quartettsatz*. Vol 7. Poetry. $7

ANTHONY JULIAN TAMBURRI, Ed. *Fuori: Essays by Italian/American Lesbiansand Gays*. Vol 6. Essays. $10

ANTONIO GRAMSCI. P. Verdicchio. Trans. & Intro. *The Southern Question*. Vol 5.Social Criticism. $5

DANIELA GIOSEFFI. *Word Wounds & Water Flowers*. Vol 4. Poetry. $8

WILEY FEINSTEIN. *Humility's Deceit: Calvino Reading Ariosto Reading Calvino*. Vol 3. Criticism. $10

PAOLO A. GIORDANO, Ed. *Joseph Tusiani: Poet. Translator. Humanist*. Vol 2. Criticism. $25

ROBERT VISCUSI. *Oration Upon the Most Recent Death of Christopher Columbus*. Vol 1. Poetry.

www.ingramcontent.com/pod-product-compliance
Lightning Source LLC
Chambersburg PA
CBHW051730040426
42447CB00008B/1066

9 781599 541358